Buckingham Palace

This is where the Queen lives. Listen for the band starting to play – you can see the Changing of the Guard some days. Watch them march!

Buckingham Palace

Changing of the Guard

Flag-waving crowd

Crown

Queen Elizabeth II

Throne

Corgi

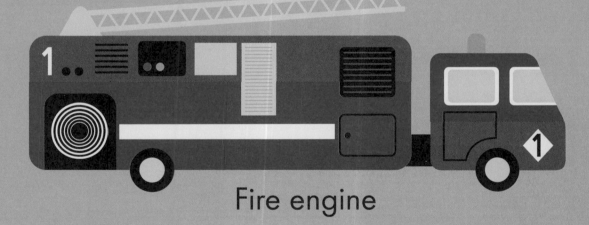

Fire engine

Royal carriage

Houses of Parliament

This historic palace is where the members of Parliament
and members of the House of Lords make laws.
Can you see Number 10 Downing Street?
The Prime Minister lives there.

News helicopter

Big Ben

Houses of Parliament

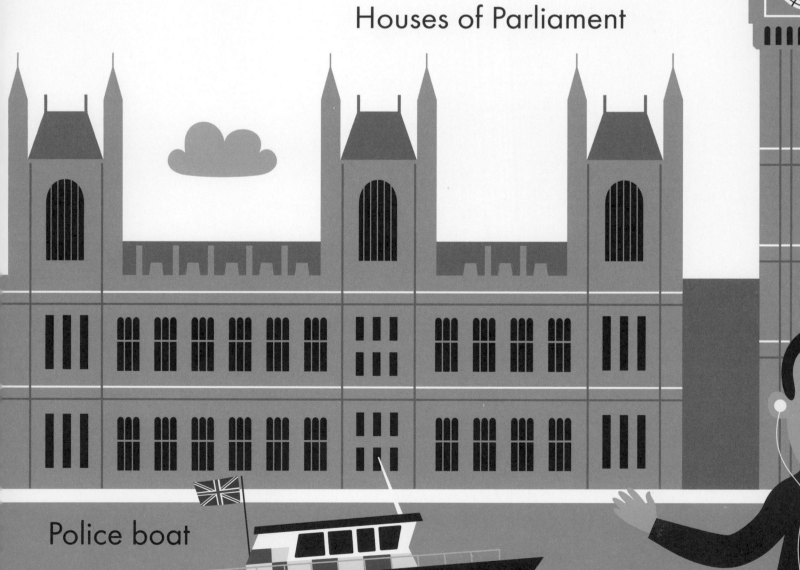

Police boat

POLICE

Reporter

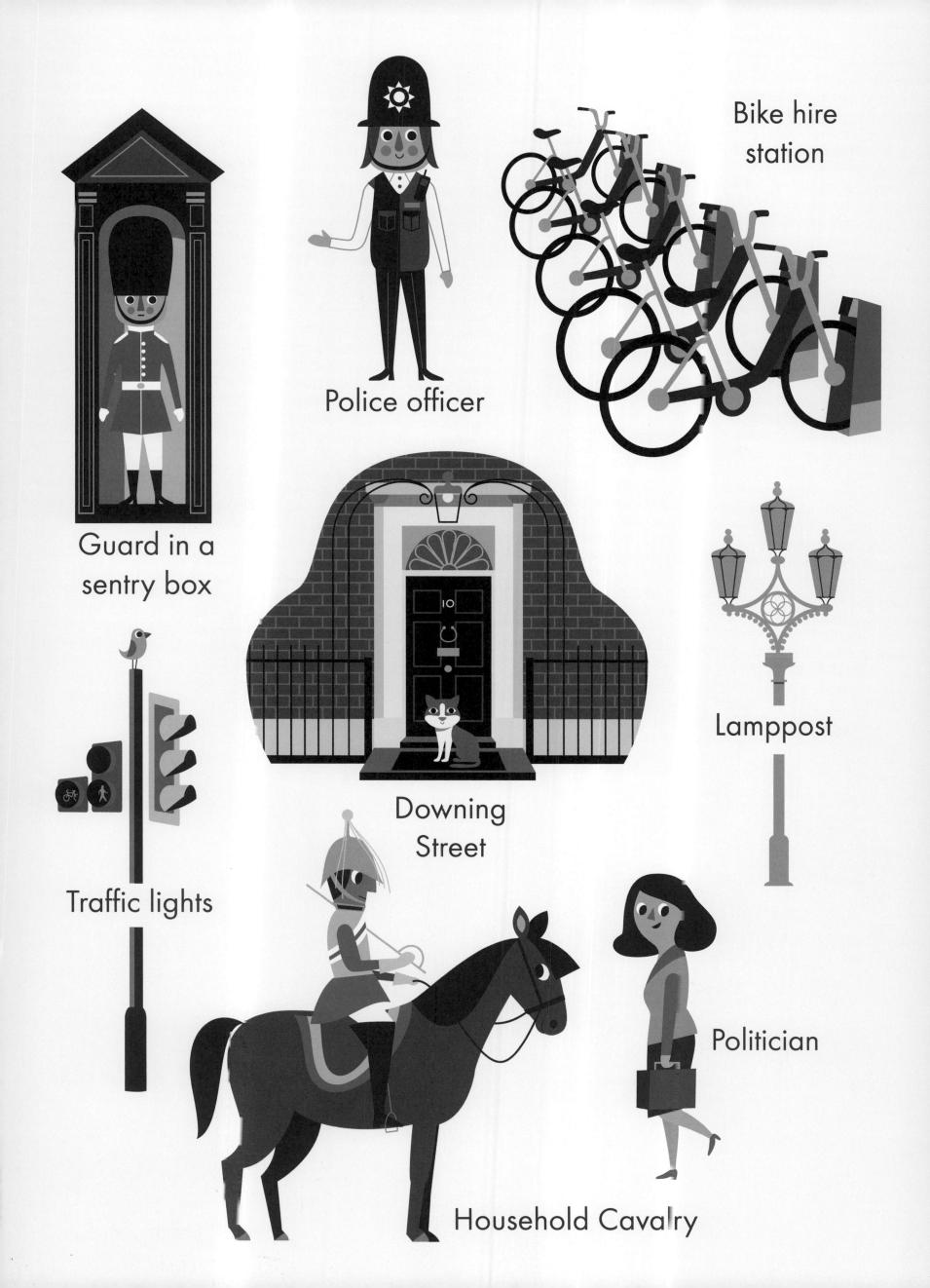

Guard in a sentry box

Police officer

Bike hire station

Downing Street

Lamppost

Traffic lights

Household Cavalry

Politician

TOWER OF LONDON

The precious Crown Jewels are locked up tight at the Tower. Look out for the Beefeaters and ravens on guard!

Tower of London

Traitors' Gate

Tower Bridge

Beefeater

Cyclist

Balloon

Ravens

Suit of armour

Crown Jewels

THE GLOBE

The first Globe Theatre built on this spot was where William Shakespeare put on many of his plays in the early 1600s. You can still watch them here today, or visit the Tate Modern next door to see the collection of modern art.

Globe Theatre

Ice-cream seller

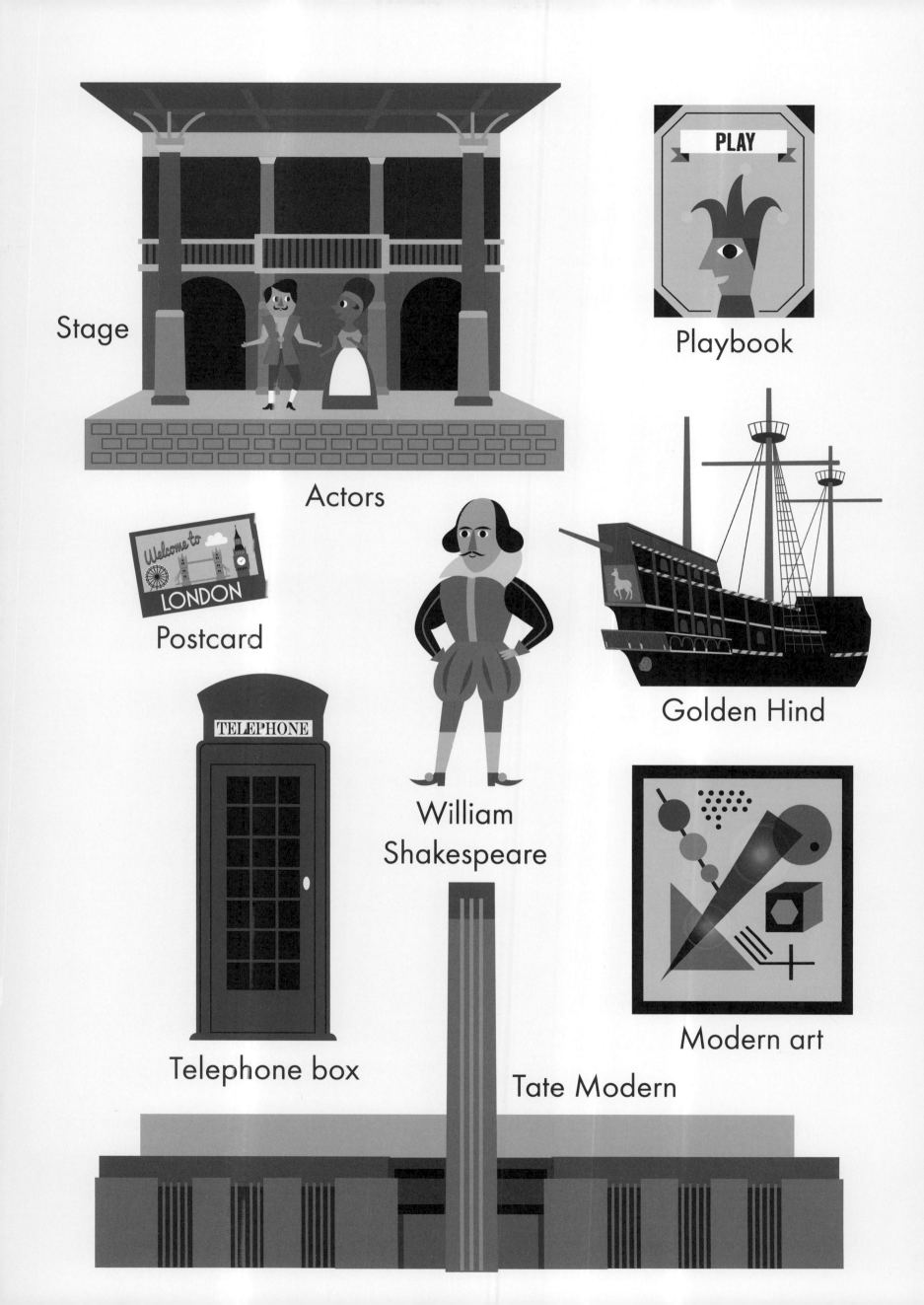

Stage

Actors

Playbook

Postcard

Golden Hind

Telephone box

William Shakespeare

Tate Modern

Modern art

LONDON ZOO

From tiny, fluttering butterflies to roaring lions, there's so much to see at the zoo. What animals can you spot? Which is your favourite?

Balloon animal

Picnic table

Zebra

Penguins

Okapi

Pelican

Giraffes

Tiger

Tortoise

Gorilla

Butterfly

Lion

Trafalgar Square

There are always lots of people here – it's the most famous square in London. Marches and rallies often start or end here.

Nelson's Column

National Gallery

Lion statue

Painting

Full English breakfast

Tourist

Pigeons

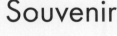

Busker

Souvenir

Fountain

HYDE PARK

This huge park's Serpentine lake is popular with swimmers and boaters. If you prefer staying dry, you can listen to a concert in the Albert Hall – the BBC Proms take place here.

Albert Hall

Albert Memorial

Picnic

Kensington Palace

Speakers' Corner

Frisbee

Diana Memorial Fountain

Horse rider

Swimmers

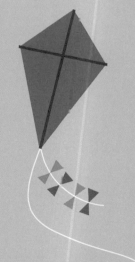
Kite

Boats on the Serpentine

LONDON EYE

From the top of this big wheel on the bank of the River Thames you can enjoy great views over the city. Why not see a show at the National Theatre nearby?

London Eye

Food market

Seagulls

Jogger

National Theatre

Bookstall

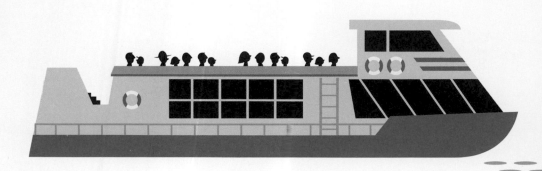

Riverboat

Skateboarder

Aquarium

SHOPPING

Toys, fashion, treats and gifts – London has shops that sell everything. You might need to stop for afternoon tea!

Harrods

Shoppers

Liberty

Afternoon tea

Postbox

WELCOME TO CARNABY STREET

Carnaby Street

Shopping bags

TOYS   HAMLEYS   TOYS

Hamleys

Covent Garden

There's something here for everyone – shops, restaurants, cafes and more. Catch a show at one of the theatres or watch one of the street performers in the plaza.

COVENT GARDEN MARKET

Plaza

Accordion player

Cafe

Theatres

Theatre programme

Street performer

Flower stall

Chinatown

London Transport Museum

QUEEN ELIZABETH OLYMPIC PARK

This is where London's Olympic and Paralympic Games were held in 2012. The stadium is now home to a football club, but you can still watch different sports here – or try some yourself.

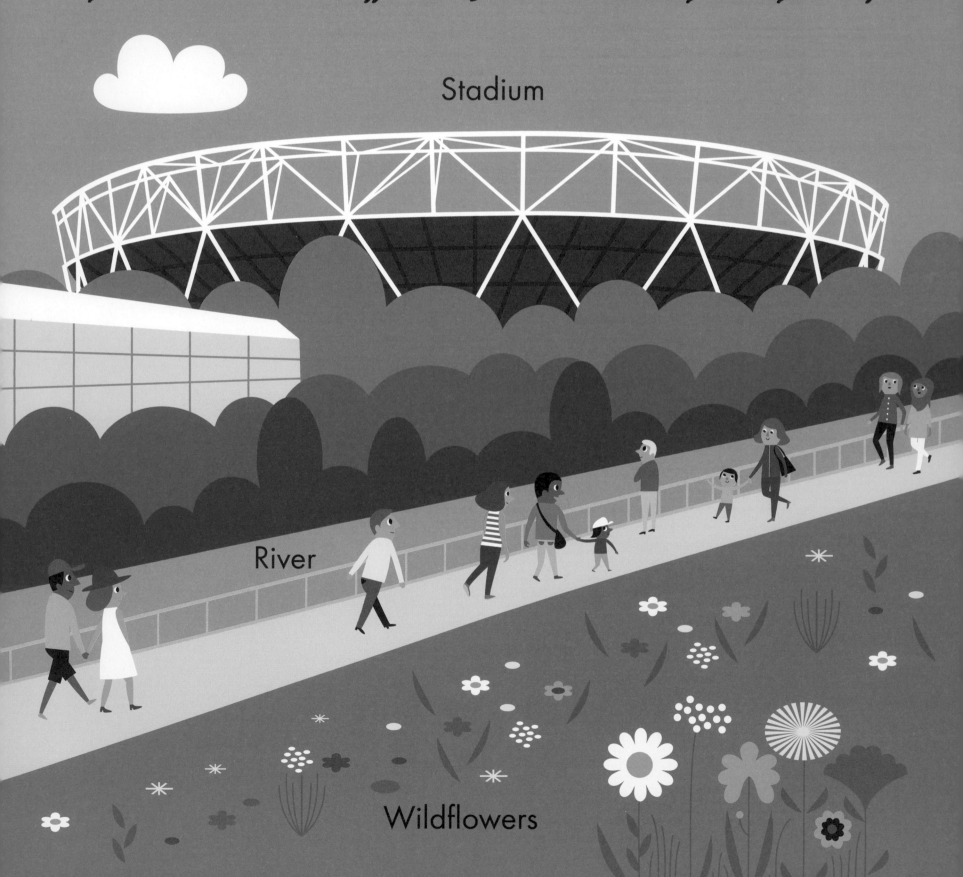

Stadium

River

Wildflowers

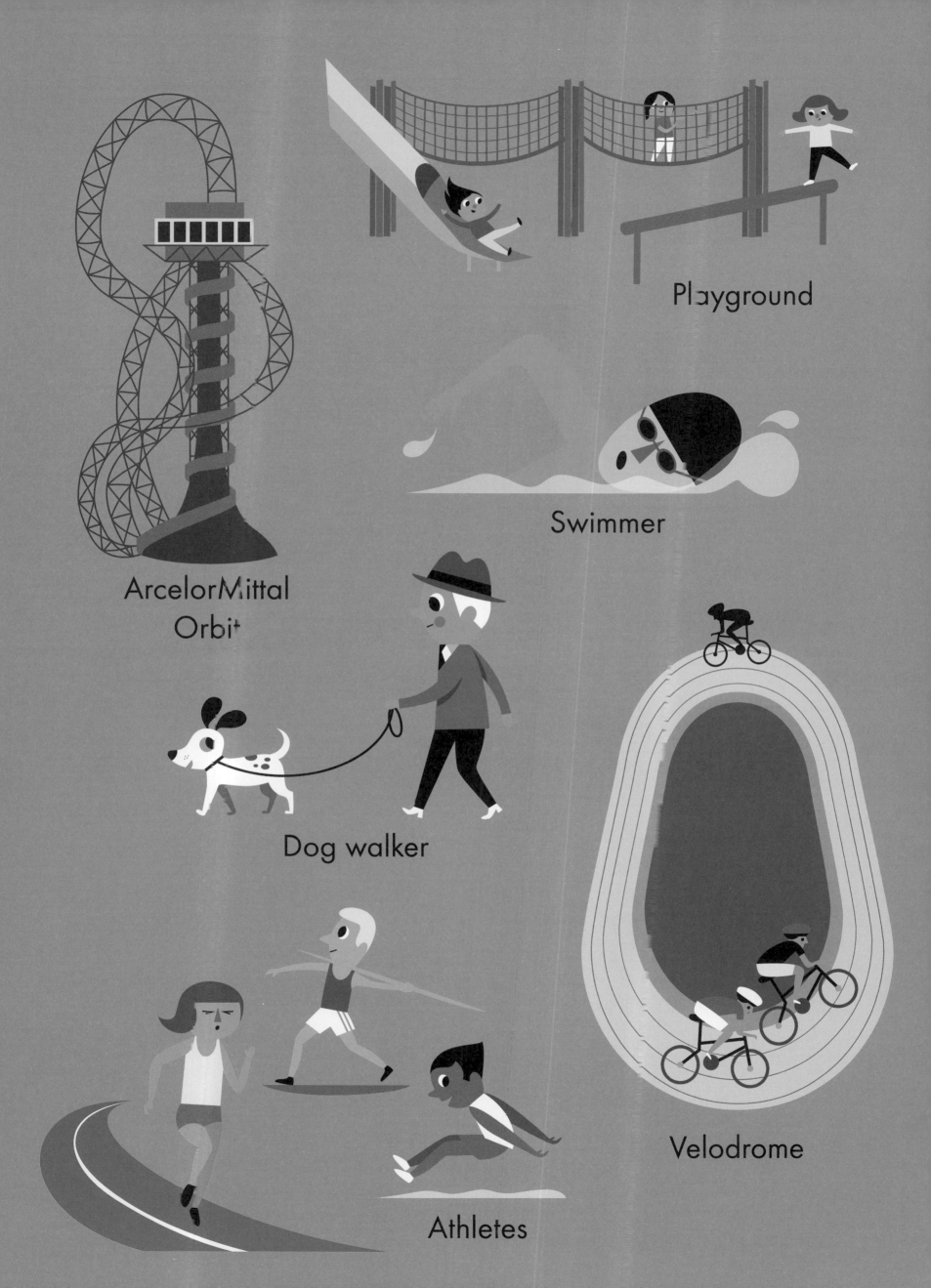

Playground

Swimmer

ArcelorMittal
Orbit

Dog walker

Velodrome

Athletes

Museums

Whether you're interested in history, science or art, you'll be amazed by the wonders on display in London's museums.

Natural History Museum

Schoolchildren

Dinosaur skeleton

V&A Museum

Terracotta vase

Egyptian
mummy

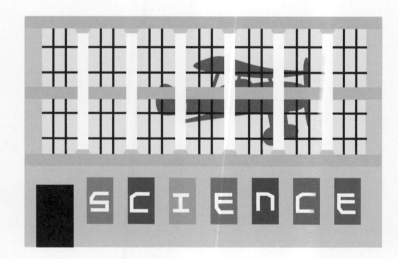

Science Museum

Rocket

British Museum

ST PAUL'S
CATHEDRAL

This cathedral is one of the most famous sights on the London skyline. Climb more than 500 steps up into its dome, and look out at all the tall skyscrapers filled with city workers.

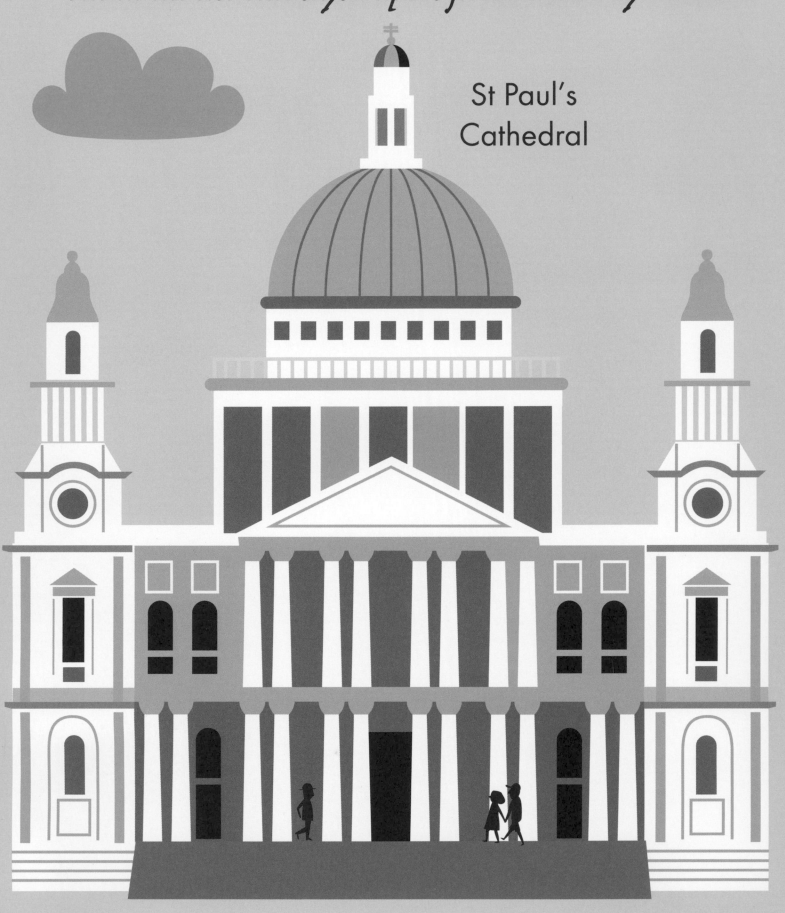

St Paul's
Cathedral

Tour guide

Bank of England

High-rise building

Construction workers

Monument to
the Great Fire of
London

Newspaper seller

Office workers

Millennium Bridge

Greenwich

Astronomers look through telescopes up at the stars from the Royal Observatory here. In the park you might spot deer, or you could visit the historic Cutty Sark down by the river.

Royal Observatory

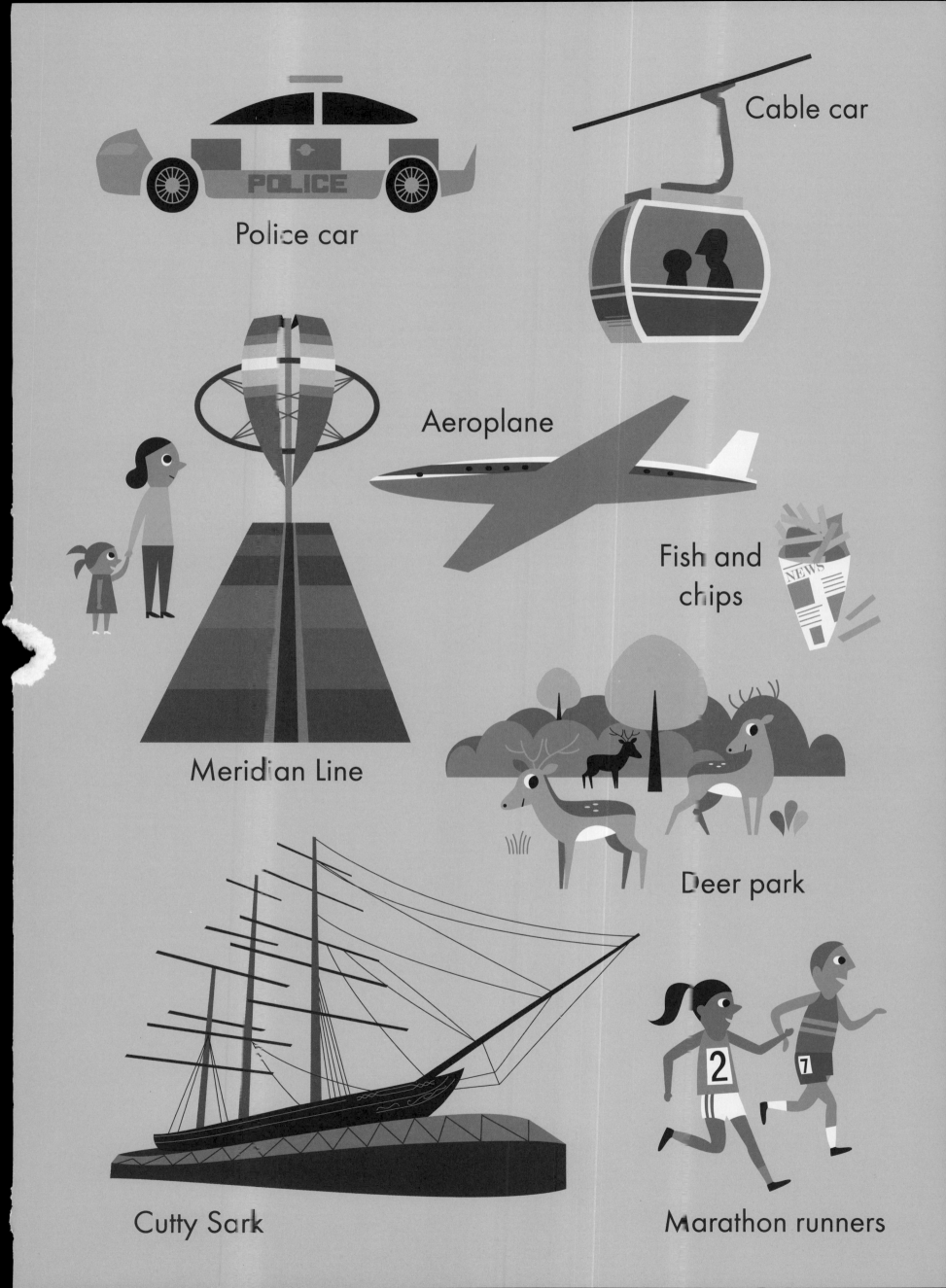

Police car

Cable car

Aeroplane

Fish and chips

Meridian Line

Deer park

Cutty Sark

Marathon runners

Piccadilly Circus

Several roads filled with traffic lead to Piccadilly Circus, a popular meeting place. It's always busy here under the bright adverts and flashing lights.

GOOD FOOD

Nice

Stuff

Eros statue